GW00992167

Cologne Cat... ...

Travel Guide 2024

Unveiling the Hidden Gems: Cologne

Cathedral Travel Guide Adventures

Folly Ray

© Copyright 2024. All Rights Reserved

In no way is it legal to reproduce, duplicate, or transmit any part of this document in either electronic means or printed format. Recording of this publication is strictly prohibited, and any storage of this document is not allowed unless with written permission from the publisher — all rights reserved.

Except for the inclusion of brief quotations in a review.

TABLE OF CONTENT

1.0 INTRODUCTION TO COLOGNE CATHEDRAL

The Cologne Cathedral, a sublime masterpiece of human ingenuity, is a towering tribute to artistic brilliance and historical legacy. Its colossal spires pierce the sky, capturing the imagination of all who gaze upon its grandeur. As one of Europe's most exceptional cathedrals, it exudes an air of solemn reverence, embodying centuries of devotion, craftsmanship, and cultural significance.

1.1 WELCOME TO COLOGNE CATHEDRAL.

Welcome to the Timeless Majesty of the Cologne Cathedral

Dear Adventurers,

Welcome, intrepid wanderers, to the hilarious and historically vibrant world of Cologne Cathedral. I'm Folly Ray, your trusty guide to the marvel that is this towering masterpiece. Now, you might be wondering, 'Why trust someone named Folly to guide us?' Well, because life is too short to be serious, especially when exploring a colossal Gothic wonder like Cologne Cathedral.

In this book, I've sprinkled more laughs than confetti at a carnival, and I promise you won't need a degree in medieval architecture to enjoy the ride. We're here to embark on a journey through time, and space, and a few quirky anecdotes that might make you snort-laugh in public places. Cologne Cathedral is not just about stones and spires; it's about the weird, the wonderful, and the downright wacky tales that history forgot to mention.

So, grab your map, your sense of humor, and maybe a pair of comfy shoes (because those medieval builders didn't think much about stiletto-friendly floors), and let's dive into the enchanting world of Cologne Cathedral. Spoiler alert: We might encounter gargoyles with a sense of humor, architects with a flair for the dramatic, and a few pigeons who think they're the real VIPs of this architectural fiesta. Get ready for a journey that's part history, part comedy show, and entirely unforgettable.

With warm regards,

Your Cologne Cathedral Adventure Awaits with Folly Ray.

1.2 OVERVIEW OF COLOGNE

Where History and Modernity Embrace

Nestled along the banks of the mighty Rhine River, Cologne, or Köln in German, stands as a vibrant testament to the harmonious blend of history, culture, and contemporary living. With a lineage dating back over 2,000 years, this city has evolved into a dynamic metropolis while preserving its rich heritage.

Historical Tapestry:

Cologne's history unfolds like a tapestry, woven with threads of Roman influence, medieval grandeur, and tales of resilience after World War II. The iconic Cologne Cathedral, a UNESCO World Heritage site, dominates the skyline with its Gothic spires and intricate architecture. This colossal masterpiece took six centuries to complete and remains a symbol of both spiritual and architectural achievement.

The city's Roman legacy is palpable in structures like the Romanesque church of Great St. Martin and remnants of the ancient city walls. Exploring the Altstadt (Old Town) reveals narrow cobblestone streets, medieval houses, and charming squares that transport visitors to a bygone era.

Cultural Kaleidoscope:

Beyond its historical allure, Cologne pulsates with a vibrant cultural scene. Museums such as the Museum Ludwig, renowned for its contemporary art collection, and the Wallraf-Richartz Museum, housing masterpieces from the Middle Ages to the 19th century, cater to diverse artistic tastes.

The city's love for music is celebrated in the Cologne Philharmonic Hall, a modern architectural gem that hosts classical and contemporary performances. Meanwhile, the annual Cologne Carnival transforms the streets into a kaleidoscope of colors, music, and exuberant festivities, reflecting the city's spirited joie de vivre.

Rhine River Magic:

The Rhine River, a lifeline for the city, provides not just a picturesque backdrop but also opportunities for scenic cruises and strolls along the riverbanks. The Hohenzollern Bridge, adorned with countless love locks, offers panoramic views of the cityscape and the cathedral.

Modern Urban Vibe:

Cologne seamlessly blends its historical charm with a modern urban vibe. The Rheinauhafen district, once an industrial hub, has transformed into a trendy waterfront area featuring contemporary architecture, stylish boutiques, and waterfront cafes. The city's commitment to sustainability is evident in initiatives like the Green Belt, a network of parks and green spaces that crisscross the urban landscape.

Culinary Delights:

Cologne's culinary scene mirrors its diverse and cosmopolitan atmosphere. From traditional beer gardens serving Kölsch, the local beer, to international fine dining establishments, the city caters to every palate. The Belgian Quarter, brimming with eclectic eateries and trendy bars showcases the city's gastronomic diversity.

In Cologne, each step is a journey through time, a harmonious symphony of ancient and modern notes playing in unison. Whether admiring the Gothic spires of the cathedral, savoring the flavors of local cuisine, or simply strolling along the Rhine, this city invites visitors to explore its multifaceted charm and discover why Cologne is not just a destination but an experience.

1.3 CATHEDRAL'S SIGNIFICANCE AND HISTORY

Cologne Cathedral: A Divine Symphony in Stone and Spirit

Significance:

Cologne Cathedral, or Kölner Dom, stands as a resplendent symbol of faith, architectural mastery, and resilience. As one of Europe's most iconic cathedrals, its significance extends beyond religious reverence, capturing the hearts of locals and visitors alike. The cathedral's towering spires dominate the skyline of Cologne, inviting awe and admiration for its Gothic grandeur.

Architectural Marvel:

Constructed over six centuries, from 1248 to 1880, Cologne Cathedral is a testament to the unwavering dedication of countless artisans, architects, and builders. The cathedral's exterior is adorned with a wealth of intricate details, from delicate tracery to gargoyles that seem to come to life against the backdrop of the sky. The soaring spires, reaching heights of 157 meters, make the cathedral the second-tallest in Germany, a marvel of medieval engineering.

Spiritual Center:
Cologne Cathedral is not merely a physical structure but the spiritual heart of the city. Its interior is a sanctuary of hallowed space, with soaring vaulted ceilings, ornate stained glass windows, and a sense of sacred silence that transcends time. The Shrine of the Three Kings, a magnificent reliquary, houses the remains of the Biblical Magi, making the cathedral an important pilgrimage site.

Cultural Heritage:
Listed as a UNESCO World Heritage site, Cologne Cathedral is a living repository of art,

history, and cultural heritage. The cathedral's rich tapestry includes masterpieces like the Twelve Choir Windows, the High Altar triptych, and the exquisite medieval sculptures that adorn its façade. The combination of these artistic elements makes the cathedral a treasure trove for art enthusiasts and historians.

Resilience Through Time:
The cathedral's history is marked by challenges, including interruptions in construction, damage during World War II, and the threat of decay. However, its resilience shines through, with ongoing restoration efforts ensuring the preservation of this architectural jewel. The intricate process of cleaning and conserving the cathedral's stone façade is a testament to modern craftsmanship preserving the legacy of the past.

Cultural Symbolism:
Beyond its religious and historical significance, Cologne Cathedral is a cultural symbol embodying the spirit of the city. Its

enduring presence through centuries of change reflects Cologne's ability to seamlessly blend tradition with a dynamic, modern identity. The cathedral's silhouette against the Rhine River is a familiar and comforting sight, a silent witness to the city's evolution.

Cologne Cathedral's significance goes beyond its physical structure; it resonates as a spiritual beacon, an architectural masterpiece, and a cultural emblem. As visitors marvel at its grandeur, they become part of a timeless narrative that connects the past, present, and future—a narrative written in stone, stained glass, and the collective spirit of those who have found solace beneath its sacred arches.

2.0 PLANNING YOUR VISIT TO COLOGNE CATHEDRAL

Embarking on a journey to Cologne Cathedral is a delightful venture, but choosing the right time enhances the overall experience. Here's a guide to help you plan your visit:

2.1 BEST TIME TO VISIT

Peak Tourist Seasons:

Cologne Cathedral welcomes visitors throughout the year, but there are peak tourist seasons when the city is bustling with activity. These high-demand periods usually coincide with:

Spring (April to June): Mild weather and blooming surroundings make spring an ideal time. However, expect larger crowds.

Summer (July to August): Warm temperatures draw more tourists. Consider early morning or late afternoon visits to avoid midday crowds.

December (Christmas Markets): The enchanting Christmas markets around the cathedral attract many visitors during the festive season. The cathedral is beautifully illuminated, creating a magical atmosphere.

Off-Peak and Shoulder Seasons:

For a more tranquil experience with shorter queues and a chance to appreciate the cathedral's details, consider visiting during:

Fall (September to November): Crisp weather and autumnal colors offer a scenic backdrop. Tourist numbers tend to decrease compared to the summer months.

Winter (January to March): While colder, this period experiences fewer crowds. The cathedral's interior, with its warm glow, can be particularly captivating during the winter months.

Weekday vs. Weekend:
Choosing the right day of the week can impact your visit:

Weekdays: If possible, plan your visit on a weekday, especially Tuesday to Thursday. These days typically have fewer tourists compared to the weekends.

Weekends: While weekends are busier, they can offer a livelier atmosphere. Consider arriving early in the morning or later in the afternoon to avoid peak midday crowds.

Special Events:

Check the calendar for any special events or religious ceremonies at the cathedral. Attending a service or event can provide a unique and culturally enriching experience.

Weather Considerations:

Cologne experiences a temperate climate, but weather conditions can influence your visit. Check the weather forecast and dress accordingly, especially if you plan to explore the outdoor areas around the cathedral.

Choosing the best time to visit Cologne Cathedral depends on your preferences and priorities. Whether you opt for a vibrant summer day, a serene winter afternoon, or the festive atmosphere of Christmas markets, each season brings its charm to this architectural marvel.

2.2 ENTRY TICKETS AND GUIDED TOURS

To step beyond the threshold of history and into the cathedral's embrace, you'll need an entry ticket. Various options are available, ranging from standard entry to combined tickets that grant access to the treasury and other areas of interest. Online ticket booking is recommended, as it helps you avoid long queues, ensuring you can spend more time immersed in the cathedral's splendor.

For those seeking a deeper understanding of the cathedral's significance, guided tours are a splendid choice. Knowledgeable guides will unravel the layers of history, art, and spirituality that enshroud the cathedral. Through their narratives, you'll gain insights that are often missed when exploring independently.

2.3 ACCESSIBILITY AND VISITOR FACILITIES

The Cologne Cathedral is committed to ensuring that every visitor can experience its magnificence. Accessibility is facilitated through ramps and designated entrances, allowing wheelchair users and those with limited mobility to explore the sacred space. Inside, well-marked pathways and elevators ensure that every corner of the cathedral is accessible.

Visitor facilities cater to the comfort of those who journey here. Restrooms, prayer rooms, and a visitor center are strategically located to ensure your needs are met. Take advantage of these amenities to enhance your visit and fully immerse yourself in the experience.

Before you embark on your pilgrimage, it's wise to check the cathedral's official website for updated information on opening hours, ticket prices, and any special events that might coincide with your visit. By meticulously planning your visit, you pave the way for a journey that will resonate deeply and leave you with memories to cherish for a lifetime.

In the next section of this guide, we'll delve into the transportation options that will lead you to the doorstep of this magnificent edifice, ensuring that your journey is as seamless as your exploration within its walls.

3.0 HOW TO GET TO COLOGNE CATHEDRAL

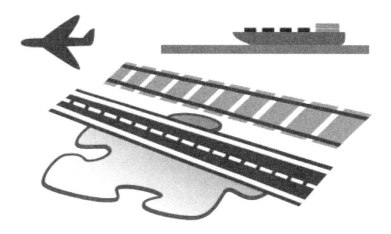

The journey to the Cologne Cathedral is not just about arriving at a destination; it's a pilgrimage into the heart of history and art. Navigating the path to this iconic monument is an integral part of your experience. From various transportation options to finding the perfect nearby accommodations, here's a comprehensive guide to ensure your journey is as enchanting as the destination itself.

3.1 TRANSPORTATION OPTIONS

Trains:

Cologne's central location makes it easily accessible by train. The Cologne Central Station (Köln Hauptbahnhof) is a major railway hub, well-connected to both national and international destinations. High-speed trains like ICE and Thalys offer a swift and scenic ride to the city. From the station, a leisurely walk or a short tram ride will lead you to the cathedral's doorstep.

Buses:

If you prefer bus travel, Cologne boasts an extensive network of regional and intercity buses. The central bus station (ZOB Köln) is conveniently located near the central train station, making it a viable option for travelers.

Flights:

If your journey begins from afar, the **Cologne Bonn Airport** provides a seamless connection to the city. Situated just 15 kilometers from the city center, the airport is well-connected to major European cities.

From the airport, a quick train ride or a taxi will swiftly transport you to the cathedral.

3.2 NEARBY ACCOMMODATIONS

As you plan your stay in Cologne, a plethora of accommodations await, catering to every preference and budget.

Hotels:

The city offers a range of hotels, from luxurious establishments that exude elegance to charming boutique hotels that capture the essence of Cologne's history.

Staying near the cathedral itself grants you the privilege of being within walking distance of this architectural marvel.

Guesthouses and Bed and Breakfasts:

For those seeking a more intimate experience, consider staying in a guesthouse or a bed and breakfast. These options often provide a cozy, personalized environment that complements the warmth of the city.

Hostels:

Travelers on a budget can find comfort and camaraderie in Cologne's hostels. These establishments offer shared dormitory-style accommodations, making them an ideal choice for solo travelers and those looking to connect with fellow explorers.

Apartment Rentals:

Embrace the feeling of being a local by opting for an apartment rental. This choice not only provides you with a home away from home but also allows you to immerse yourself in the neighborhoods of Cologne.

Final Tips:

Regardless of your chosen accommodation, proximity to public transportation and the cathedral is a valuable factor to consider. Exploring the city's charm extends beyond the cathedral, and easy access to transportation hubs ensures that you can effortlessly explore Cologne's other treasures.

As you journey to the Cologne Cathedral, let the path you choose to travel be as significant as the destination itself. Whether you arrive by train, bus, or plane, and wherever you rest your head, know that each step is an integral part of your pilgrimage—a journey that will forever connect you to the grandeur of history and the elegance of art that awaits within the cathedral's walls.

4.0 EXPLORING THE CATHEDRAL

Your journey to the Cologne Cathedral culminates in an opportunity to step into the pages of history and immerse yourself in the splendor of human achievement. The cathedral's architecture is a symphony of stone, an intricate dance of light and shadow, and a testament to the boundless creativity of the human spirit. As you embark on this exploration, prepare to be captivated by the architectural highlights that adorn every corner of this awe-inspiring edifice.

4.1 ARCHITECTURAL HIGHLIGHTS

Gothic Majesty:

The Cologne Cathedral is an exemplar of High Gothic architecture, characterized by its soaring verticality and intricate details. The façade itself is a marvel, with its twin spires reaching heights that seem to touch the heavens. As you stand before this majestic facade, allow your gaze to trace the delicate tracery, the ornate sculptures, and the meticulous craftsmanship that tell stories of devotion and artistry.

Stunning Stained Glass:

Venture inside, and you'll be greeted by a kaleidoscope of colors streaming through the cathedral's stunning stained glass windows. These windows are not just artistic marvels; they're a spiritual narrative told through vivid hues.

The south transept window, known as the "Window of the Last Judgment," is particularly striking, depicting scenes of salvation and damnation in breathtaking detail.

Sculptural Extravaganza:

Every niche, arch, and column within the cathedral is adorned with sculptures that bring to life a pantheon of saints, biblical figures, and allegorical representations. **The "Milan Madonna,"**

a wooden sculpture located in the crossing, is a masterpiece of medieval sculpture. As you traverse the cathedral, take the time to appreciate the intricacy of these sculptures, which stand as testaments to the skill and devotion of the artisans.

Ambulatory and Chapels:

The ambulatory, the walkway that encircles the main altar, provides a unique perspective on the cathedral's architecture. Here, you can marvel at the ribbed vaults that seem to hold up the heavens themselves. The chapels that punctuate the ambulatory are individual works of art, each with its own story to tell. The Shrine of the Three Kings, an opulent golden reliquary, is a highlight, believed to hold the remains of the Three Wise Men.

Organ and Nave:

The grandeur of the nave, with its towering columns and high vaulted ceilings, is an experience in itself. It's home to one of the largest free-swinging church bells in the world, the "Peter Bell," which tolls with a resonance that can be felt deep within. The awe-inspiring Klais organ, with its 86 stops and over 7000 pipes, adds a musical dimension to the cathedral's aura.

Every step you take within the Cologne Cathedral is a brushstroke in a masterpiece that spans centuries. The architectural highlights you encounter are not just structures; they're a visual symphony that invites you to witness the harmonious blend of faith and creativity. As you explore each intricate detail, remember that you're engaging with a legacy that has been carefully preserved across time—a legacy that stands as a tribute to the infinite potential of human imagination and dedication.

4.2 NAVIGATING THE INTERIOR AND EXTERIOR OF COLOGNE CATHEDRAL

Stepping into the Cologne Cathedral is akin to entering a sacred labyrinth of history, art, and spirituality. The interior and exterior of this awe-inspiring edifice hold secrets waiting to be uncovered, stories eager to be shared, and a journey that promises to enrich your soul. Let's delve into how to navigate the intricate beauty of both the cathedral's inner sanctum and its awe-inspiring façade.

Navigating the Interior:

Central Nave:

The heart of the cathedral is its central nave, a vast expanse that stretches towards the heavens. As you walk along this grand corridor, allow yourself to be enveloped by the soaring columns and ribbed vaults that create a sense of verticality. Marvel at the play of light and shadow, which cast an ethereal glow upon the intricate details.

Side Aisles and Chapels:

The side aisles are home to chapels adorned with sculptures, altars, and artwork. Each chapel has a unique story to tell, from the richly ornamented Chapel of St. Agilolfus to the serene Chapel of the Cross. Take your time to explore these hidden gems, as they offer intimate glimpses into the cathedral's spiritual and artistic tapestry.

Ambulatory and Transepts: The ambulatory encircles the main altar, offering a pathway for reflection and contemplation. This space leads to the transepts, where you'll find the crossing beneath the central tower. Look up to witness the intricate ribbed vaulting that converges here, seemingly holding up the weight of centuries.

Navigating the Exterior:

Facade and Portals:

The exterior facade is an intricate canvas that tells stories through sculpture. The portals, such as the Portal of the Last Judgment, are adorned with intricate carvings that depict scenes from the Bible. Take your time to decipher the narratives and appreciate the artistry that adorns the cathedral's entrance.

Towers and Spires:

The twin spires of the cathedral are its crowning glory, soaring above the city skyline. While visitors can't ascend these spires, gazing up at their intricate details from the ground is an experience in itself. The South Tower offers guided tours for those who wish to venture up and witness panoramic views of the city.

4.3 VIEWING PLATFORMS AND PANORAMAS

For those seeking to ascend the heights of the Cologne Cathedral, a rewarding experience awaits. The South Tower, known as the "Domglocke," offers guided tours that lead you up a series of narrow staircases to breathtaking panoramic views. As you ascend, you'll catch glimpses of the cathedral's inner workings, offering a unique perspective on its architecture.

Upon reaching the viewing platform, the sprawling city of Cologne stretches before you, revealing its modern vibrancy alongside historic landmarks. The River Rhine winds its way through the landscape, adding to the visual spectacle. With the cathedral's intricate stonework beneath your feet and the city spread out before you, you'll feel a sense of unity between past and present.

Remember that climbing the tower requires physical stamina, as the staircases can be narrow and steep. However, the effort is rewarded with an unforgettable vantage point that provides a new dimension to your understanding of the cathedral's place within the urban fabric of Cologne.

In your exploration of the cathedral's interior and exterior, you're embarking on a dialogue with history and architecture—an exchange that invites you to be an active participant in the cathedral's narrative. As you navigate its labyrinthine spaces and ascend to its heights, you're not just observing; you're engaging with the essence of the Cologne Cathedral—a living testament to human aspiration, devotion, and artistic brilliance.

5.0 CULTURAL INSIGHTS IN COLOGNE CATHEDRAL

The Cologne Cathedral is not merely a stone edifice; it is a repository of cultural treasures that speak to the human spirit's boundless capacity for creation and devotion. Within its hallowed halls and beneath its soaring spires, a tapestry of historical context, architectural marvels, and vibrant cultural events unfolds, inviting visitors to become a part of its rich legacy.

5.1 HISTORICAL CONTEXT AND CONSTRUCTION FACTS

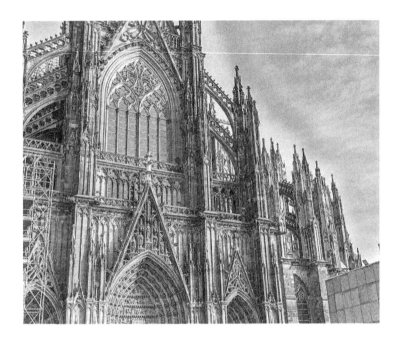

The roots of the Cologne Cathedral extend deep into history. Its construction began in 1248, a period when the Gothic architectural style was taking Europe by storm. Intended as a testament to faith, it wasn't until the 19th century that the cathedral's completion was realized. The intricate process of construction was punctuated by the dedication of generations of builders, architects, and artists who invested their creativity, skill, and devotion into bringing this monumental vision to life.

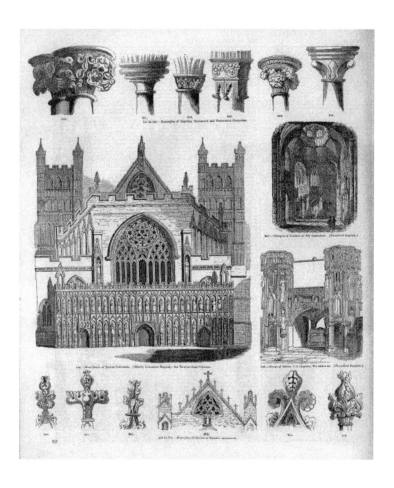

The Cologne Cathedral survived the ravages of time and wars. During World War II, the cathedral withstood heavy bombing raids that devastated much of the city. Its resilience in the face of destruction became a symbol of hope for the people of Cologne. Today, its enduring presence stands as a testament to human perseverance and the power of faith and culture to transcend adversity.

5.2 CULTURAL EVENTS AND EXHIBITIONS

The cathedral isn't just a relic of the past; it's a living cultural entity that continues to evolve with the times. Throughout the year, a diverse array of events and exhibitions breathe new life into its ancient spaces. These events bridge the gap between history and contemporary culture, inviting visitors to engage with the cathedral on multiple levels.

Concerts and Music Performances: The cathedral's acoustics lend themselves to soul-stirring musical performances. Concerts featuring choirs, orchestras, and soloists transform the sacred space into a stage for artistic expression. Whether it's a rendition of classical compositions or a celebration of local folk music, these performances merge history with the present, creating an enchanting experience.

Religious Ceremonies: The cathedral remains a vibrant hub of religious life, hosting worship services, ceremonies, and processions. Participating in a mass within its walls allows visitors to connect with the cathedral's spiritual legacy and experience the living heartbeat of its culture.

Art Exhibitions: Various exhibitions are held within the cathedral precincts, showcasing contemporary art that complements the historical surroundings. These exhibitions create a dialogue between the old and the new, sparking conversations about the evolving role of art and culture in society.

Special Cultural Events:

The Cologne Cathedral often hosts events that celebrate local traditions, holidays, and cultural festivals. From Christmas markets that evoke a sense of wonder to processions that honor the city's patron saints, these events immerse visitors in the city's living heritage.

In engaging with the cathedral's cultural insights, you're not just observing history; you're participating in a dynamic conversation that spans centuries. The historical context and construction facts provide a backdrop against which the present-day cultural events and exhibitions come to life. By experiencing these cultural facets, you're not just a visitor; you become a part of the cathedral's continuing narrative—a narrative that binds past, present, and future in a seamless tapestry of human creativity and aspiration.

6.0 RELIGIOUS SIGNIFICANCE OF COLOGNE CATHEDRAL

The Cologne Cathedral isn't solely a monument of architectural splendor; it's a spiritual sanctuary that holds a profound place in the hearts of the faithful and the community. It is a living testament to devotion, faith, and the unbreakable bond between the divine and the human. The religious significance of the cathedral extends beyond its walls, encompassing its role within the community, the worship services held within, and the ceremonies that reflect the enduring spirit of Cologne's inhabitants.

6.1 ROLE OF THE CATHEDRAL IN THE COMMUNITY

The cathedral's spires reach far beyond the physical realm; they touch the spiritual aspirations of the community. For centuries, the Cologne Cathedral has been more than a place of worship; it's a unifying symbol that transcends differences and fosters a sense of belonging among the people. It's where generations have come to seek solace, find answers, and forge connections with something greater than themselves.

As a cultural epicenter, the cathedral has witnessed the milestones of the city's history. From joyful celebrations to somber commemorations, it has been a silent witness to the ebb and flow of human experience. In times of celebration, its bells have rung out in triumph. In times of adversity, its presence has provided a haven of solace. Its role goes beyond the individual; it's a collective emblem that unites the community under the banner of shared faith and shared humanity.

6.2 WORSHIP SERVICES AND CEREMONIES

The cathedral pulsates with religious life, hosting a spectrum of worship services and ceremonies that reflect the diverse facets of faith. Daily masses, held in various languages, provide opportunities for the devout to engage in communal prayer and reflection. These services bridge the gap between the sacred and the secular, weaving spirituality into the fabric of daily life.

Throughout the liturgical calendar, the cathedral comes alive with ceremonies that mark the milestones of faith. From baptisms that welcome new members into the community to weddings that bind souls in matrimony, these ceremonies are a testament to the enduring traditions that have thrived within the cathedral's walls for centuries.

Special liturgical events, such as Easter and Christmas services, draw pilgrims and visitors from around the world. These celebrations transform the cathedral into a space of transcendence, where the timeless rituals of faith unfold against the backdrop of its awe-inspiring architecture.

The Cologne Cathedral's religious significance is a thread that weaves through the city's history, culture, and identity. Its role isn't confined to one faith; it's a place where the spiritual yearnings of people from all walks of life converge. From worship services that touch the individual soul to communal ceremonies that bind the community together, the cathedral's significance is a testament to the enduring power of faith to shape lives, stories, and destinies.

7.0 THE SURROUNDING ATTRACTIONS OF COLOGNE CATHEDRAL

The Cologne Cathedral isn't an isolated marvel; it's the epicenter of a city that brims with history, culture, and beauty. As you step away from the cathedral's awe-inspiring presence, you'll find yourself surrounded by a tapestry of attractions that complement its grandeur. From museums that house treasures of art and history to the picturesque promenade along the Rhine River, the surroundings of the cathedral offer a plethora of experiences waiting to be explored.

7.1 NEARBY MUSEUMS AND LANDMARKS

Romano-Germanic-Museum:

Immerse yourself in ancient history at the Romano-Germanic Museum. This archaeological treasure trove showcases artifacts from the Roman period, allowing you to connect with Cologne's roots as a Roman colony.

Ludwig Museum:

A modern counterpart to the ancient, the Ludwig Museum is a haven for contemporary art enthusiasts. Its collection spans modern art movements, featuring works by artists like Picasso, Warhol, and Lichtenstein.

Cologne City Museum:

Delve into the city's history at the Cologne City Museum. Exhibits weave together the story of Cologne's evolution, providing insights into its cultural heritage and urban development.

Hohenzollern Bridge:

94

Cross the iconic Hohenzollern Bridge, adorned with countless love locks, offering panoramic views of the cathedral and the Rhine River. It's a romantic spot that offers a unique perspective on the cityscape.

7.2 RHINE RIVER PROMENADE

The Rhine River, a lifeline that has shaped Cologne's destiny, offers a scenic backdrop to your explorations. The Rhine River promenade is a vibrant hub of activity, where locals and visitors alike gather to soak in the atmosphere. Take a stroll along the promenade, stopping to admire the view, people-watch, or simply enjoy the breeze.

Cruise boats line the riverbanks, offering a unique vantage point from which to appreciate the city's skyline and landmarks. A river cruise provides a different perspective of the Cologne Cathedral, allowing you to appreciate its grandeur from the waters that have played a pivotal role in the city's history.

Street musicians, artists, and vendors add a touch of liveliness to the promenade, creating an ambiance that's both bustling and relaxing. Whether you're sipping coffee at a riverside café or taking in the sights from a park bench, the Rhine River promenade is a picturesque escape that complements your exploration of the cathedral.

In the heart of the city, the Cologne Cathedral is surrounded by attractions that beckon you to continue your journey of discovery. From museums that unlock the past to the serene beauty of the Rhine River promenade, the cathedral's surroundings offer a balanced blend of history, culture, and leisure that ensures your visit to Cologne is a multi-dimensional experience.

8.0 LOCAL CUISINE AND DINING OF COLOGNE CATHEDRAL

A journey to the Cologne Cathedral isn't just about exploring history and architecture; it's an opportunity to savor the flavors of the city's culinary heritage. Cologne's local cuisine is a delightful tapestry of traditional flavors and modern twists, and the area around the cathedral offers a plethora of dining options that promise to tantalize your taste buds. Let's delve into the culinary specialties of Cologne and the diverse restaurants and cafes that await you.

8.1 CULINARY SPECIALTIES OF COLOGNE

Kölsch:

Start your culinary adventure with a taste of Kölsch, the city's iconic beer. This light and crisp beer is served in small glasses, and the tradition is to continuously refill your glass unless you place a coaster over it. Many local pubs offer Kölsch, making it an integral part of the Cologne experience.

Himmel und Äd:

Translating to "Heaven and Earth," this dish is a hearty concoction of mashed potatoes (the earth) and apple puree (the heaven), topped with slices of black pudding. It's a symphony of flavors and textures that pay homage to regional ingredients.

Sauerbraten:

A German classic, sauerbraten is a pot roast usually made with beef, marinated in a mixture of vinegar or wine, and served with a rich gravy. The tangy marinade gives the dish a distinct flavor profile.

Halver Hahn:

Don't be fooled by the name; this local snack isn't half chicken. It's a rye bread roll topped with butter, cheese, mustard, and onions. It's a simple yet satisfying treat that's perfect for a quick bite.

8.2 RESTAURANTS AND CAFES AROUND THE CATHEDRAL

Früh am Dom:

This historic brewery and restaurant is a Cologne institution. Serving Kölsch in a lively atmosphere, it's a perfect spot to savor local beer and classic German dishes. The traditional ambiance and hearty food make it a favorite among both locals and visitors.

Em Krützche:

Set in a charming half-timbered building, this restaurant offers a menu that celebrates regional specialties. From sauerbraten to Himmel und Äd, you'll find a variety of dishes that showcase the culinary heritage of Cologne.

Gilden im Zims:

This restaurant combines tradition with innovation, offering a menu that blends classic Kölsch cuisine with creative twists. The cozy interior and attentive service provide a welcoming ambiance for your dining experience.

Cafés along the Rhine:

The Rhine River promenade is dotted with cafes that offer stunning views of the river and the cathedral. Whether you're sipping coffee, indulging in cake, or enjoying a leisurely meal, these cafes provide a serene setting to unwind and soak in the atmosphere.

As you explore the culinary landscape around the cathedral, you're immersing yourself in the heart of Cologne's culture. From the flavors that have been savored for generations to the modern interpretations that reflect the city's evolving tastes, the local cuisine is an essential element of your journey. So, indulge your senses and savor each bite as you experience the marriage of tradition and innovation on your palate.

9.0 SHOPPING AND SOUVENIRS IN COLOGNE CATHEDRAL

9.1 UNIQUE ITEMS TO BUY NEAR THE COLOGNE CATHEDRAL

Shopping around the Cologne Cathedral is an experience that blends history, culture, and modernity. The cathedral itself is a stunning architectural masterpiece, and the area around it offers a variety of unique items that make for great souvenirs.

Cologne Cathedral Souvenirs:

As you might expect, there are numerous souvenir shops offering items like postcards, keychains, mugs, and miniature replicas of the cathedral. These souvenirs are perfect for commemorating your visit and sharing your experience with friends and family.

Cologne Cathedral-themed Jewelry: You'll find jewelry inspired by the cathedral's intricate details. From necklaces featuring delicate spires to earrings with stained glass designs, these pieces capture the essence of the cathedral in a wearable form.

Fragrances and Perfumes: Cologne, the city, is known for its world-famous fragrance. Close to the cathedral, you can find shops offering a variety of colognes and perfumes that make for a memorable and authentic souvenir.

Cathedral-inspired Art:

The artistic beauty of the cathedral has inspired local artists to create paintings, sketches, and other forms of art that reflect its grandeur. Purchasing such art pieces can bring a touch of Cologne's culture and history to your home.

Stained Glass Artwork: The cathedral's stained glass windows are iconic. While acquiring an actual piece of stained glass might not be feasible, you can find intricate stained glass artwork that captures the beauty of the windows in a portable form.

9.2 LOCAL MARKETS AND SHOPS

The area surrounding the Cologne Cathedral is home to various local markets and shops that offer a diverse range of products, from traditional crafts to modern fashion.

Cologne Cathedral Market: In front of the cathedral, there are often small markets selling handcrafted goods, local delicacies, and artisanal items. This market atmosphere adds to the overall experience of visiting the cathedral.

Hohe Straße and Schildergasse:

These two shopping streets are located close to the cathedral and offer a mix of international brands and local boutiques. You'll find clothing, accessories, and other items here.

Eau de Cologne Shops: Since the city is famous for its cologne, you'll find dedicated shops selling an extensive range of fragrances. These shops allow you to explore and purchase scents that are unique to Cologne.

Antique Shops: If you're interested in antiques and vintage items, the area around the cathedral has several antique shops. You might stumble upon treasures that hold historical significance.

Cologne Christmas Markets: If you're visiting during the holiday season, the Christmas markets near the cathedral are a must-see. They offer an enchanting atmosphere with seasonal treats, handcrafted ornaments, and traditional gifts.

Shopping near the Cologne Cathedral provides a delightful blend of traditional and contemporary items that celebrate the city's history and culture. Whether you're looking for souvenirs, unique jewelry, fragrances, or local crafts, you'll find an array of options that capture the essence of Cologne.

10.0 PRACTICAL TIPS FOR VISITING COLOGNE CATHEDRAL

10.1 DRESS CODE AND ETIQUETTE WITHIN THE CATHEDRAL

When visiting Cologne Cathedral, it's important to be mindful of the dress code and follow proper etiquette to ensure a respectful and enjoyable experience:

Modest Attire: Since the cathedral is a place of worship, it's recommended to dress modestly. Avoid wearing revealing clothing such as short skirts, shorts, and sleeveless tops. Both men and women should consider wearing clothing that covers the shoulders and knees.

Quiet and Respectful Behavior: As a place of religious significance, visitors are expected to maintain a quiet and respectful demeanor. Speaking softly and refraining from loud conversations will help preserve the solemn atmosphere.

Photography and Videography: Photography and filming are often allowed inside the cathedral, but it's essential to confirm with the staff or signs whether it's permitted. If allowed, be discreet and avoid using flash, as it can disturb other visitors.

Flash Photography: In many cathedrals, including Cologne Cathedral, the use of flash photography is typically not allowed. Flash can damage delicate artworks, such as frescoes and stained glass, over time.

Seating Areas: If there are designated seating areas for visitors, consider sitting quietly and taking in the surroundings.

Remember that benches may be reserved for worshipers during religious services.

10.2 SAFETY AND SECURITY INFORMATION

While visiting Cologne Cathedral, prioritize your safety and the security of the historic site:

Baggage and Belongings: Avoid bringing large bags or backpacks into the cathedral, as they can be a hindrance to both you and other visitors. Some places might offer storage facilities for larger items.

Pickpocket Awareness: As with any crowded tourist destination, be cautious of pickpockets. Keep your belongings secure and consider using an anti-theft bag or wearing a money belt.

Stay Hydrated: The interior of cathedrals can get warm, especially during peak tourist seasons. Carry a bottle of water to stay hydrated, but remember to be discreet if you need to take a sip.

Emergency Exits: Take note of the emergency exits when you enter the cathedral, so you'll know how to exit quickly and safely in case of any unforeseen circumstances.

Follow Instructions: Pay attention to any instructions provided by staff or security personnel. They are there to ensure the safety and well-being of all visitors.

Health Considerations: If you have any health concerns, be aware that cathedrals can involve a lot of walking and sometimes climbing stairs. Take breaks as needed and plan your visit accordingly.

By adhering to these practical tips, you can have a respectful and safe visit to Cologne Cathedral. Being considerate of the cathedral's significance and its rules will enhance your experience and allow you to fully appreciate the beauty and history of this architectural marvel.

11.0 FREQUENTLY ASKED QUESTIONS ABOUT COLOGNE CATHEDRAL

Embarking on a journey to the historic Cologne Cathedral may spark various questions, and we're here to provide answers to some of the most commonly asked queries as of 2024:

1. What is the significance of Cologne Cathedral?

Answer: Cologne Cathedral is a monumental Gothic masterpiece with immense historical, cultural, and religious significance. It is not only a symbol of medieval architectural prowess but also houses important relics, including the Shrine of the Three Kings, making it a key pilgrimage site.

2. How tall is Cologne Cathedral?

Answer: As of 2024, Cologne Cathedral stands at a height of approximately 157 meters (515 feet), making it the second-tallest cathedral in Germany. Its twin spires dominate the city's skyline, offering breathtaking panoramic views.

3. Is there an entrance fee to visit the cathedral?

Answer: While entry to the main body of the cathedral is generally free, there may be a fee to access certain areas, such as the tower or treasury. It's advisable to check the official website or inquire locally for the most up-to-date information on entrance fees.

4. Can you climb the Cologne Cathedral towers?

Answer: Yes, visitors have the opportunity to climb the towers of Cologne Cathedral. The ascent provides not only a physical challenge but also rewards climbers with stunning views of the city and the Rhine River. Be prepared for a number of steps and narrow passages.

5. Are there guided tours available?

Answer: Guided tours are indeed available and can enhance your understanding of the cathedral's history, architecture, and cultural significance. Tours may be conducted in various languages, so it's advisable to check in advance and book if necessary.

6. What is the best time to visit Cologne Cathedral to avoid crowds?

Answer: To avoid peak crowds, consider visiting on weekdays, particularly Tuesday to Thursday. Early mornings or late afternoons are generally less busy. During off-peak seasons, such as fall or winter, visitor numbers tend to decrease.

7. Is photography allowed inside the cathedral?

Answer: Photography is generally allowed inside the main body of the cathedral for personal use. However, restrictions may apply in certain areas or during religious services. It's recommended to be respectful and check for any posted guidelines.

8. Can you attend a religious service at Cologne Cathedral?

Answer: Yes, Cologne Cathedral is an active place of worship, and visitors are welcome to attend religious services. Check the cathedral's schedule for Mass times and other religious events.

9. What is the best way to get to Cologne Cathedral?

Answer: Cologne Cathedral is centrally located in the city. You can easily reach it by public transportation, including trains and buses. If you're staying within the city, walking is a convenient option due to the cathedral's prominent position.

10. Are there dining options near Cologne Cathedral?

Answer: Yes, the vicinity around Cologne Cathedral offers a variety of dining options, ranging from traditional German cuisine to international fare. The charming cafes and restaurants provide opportunities to savor local flavors.

Cologne Cathedral, with its rich history and cultural prominence, continues to captivate visitors in 2024. These FAQs aim to guide you through the essential information, ensuring a memorable and informed visit to this architectural gem.

12.0 USEFUL CONTACTS FOR VISITORS TO COLOGNE

When visiting Cologne, it's important to have access to useful contacts for emergencies and information. Here are some essential numbers and contacts that can be helpful during your stay:

12.1 Emergency Numbers:

Emergency Services (Police, Fire, Ambulance): **112**
In case of any emergency, dial 112 to reach the appropriate emergency service. This number is valid throughout the European Union.

Police (Non-Emergency): **110**
For non-urgent police assistance or reporting incidents that don't require immediate attention, you can dial 110.

Medical Emergency: **112**
If you need urgent medical assistance, dial 112 to request an ambulance.

12.2 Tourist Information Centers:

Cologne Tourist Board: **+49 221 346 43 210**
The Cologne Tourist Board can provide information about attractions, events, accommodations, and other travel-related queries.

Cologne Tourism Information Center: Located at the Cologne Central Station (Köln Hauptbahnhof), this center offers maps, brochures, and assistance for visitors.

12.3 Embassies and Consulates:

It's also important to have the contact information of your country's embassy or consulate in case you encounter any difficulties or require assistance while abroad.

12.4 Medical Assistance:

Cologne University Hospital (Universitätsklinikum Köln): **+49 221 478-0**
In case of medical emergencies, the university hospital provides comprehensive medical care.

Pharmacies (Apotheke):
Pharmacies are widely available in Cologne. Look for the nearest one if you need over-the-counter medication or advice.

12.5 Transportation:

Public Transportation Information: For information about public transportation options, routes, and schedules, you can contact the Kölner Verkehrs-Betriebe (KVB) customer service.

12.6 Language Assistance:

If you encounter language barriers, consider having a translation app or contact information for local language schools that might offer assistance.

12.7 Lost And Found:

Cologne Lost and Found Office (Fundbüro Köln): **+49 221 221-0**
If you lose something valuable during your visit, you can inquire at the lost and found office.

Having these useful contacts at hand ensures that you're well-prepared for your trip to Cologne and can quickly access help or information if needed. Remember to save these numbers in your phone or keep them in a convenient location for easy reference.

13.0 APPENDIX

13.1 GLOSSARY OF ARCHITECTURAL TERMS

Here's a glossary of architectural terms that can help you better understand the elements of Cologne Cathedral and its design:

Gothic Architecture: A style characterized by pointed arches, ribbed vaults, and flying buttresses. Cologne Cathedral is a prime example of High Gothic architecture.

Nave: The central area of a church, often flanked by aisles, where the congregation gathers for worship.

Transept: The arms of the cross-shaped floor plan of a cruciform church. It intersects the nave, forming the shape of a cross.

Apse: A semicircular or polygonal projection at the end of a cathedral, usually housing the altar.

Stained Glass: Colored glass that has been painted and fired, creating intricate designs and images. Cathedrals often feature stunning stained glass windows.

Flying Buttress: An architectural support that extends from the exterior of a building and counteracts the lateral thrust of the vaults, allowing for taller walls and windows.

Ribbed Vault: A type of vaulting with projecting stone ribs that support the weight of the ceiling or roof.

Spire: A tall, pointed structure, often located on top of a tower. The Cologne Cathedral's spires are iconic elements of its skyline.

13.2 HISTORICAL TIMELINE OF THE CATHEDRAL

1248:

The foundation stone of Cologne Cathedral, officially known as the Cathedral Church of Saint Peter, is laid on the 15th of August. The construction is initiated under the guidance of Archbishop Konrad von Hochstaden.

1322:

After decades of progress, the construction comes to a halt due to insufficient funds and resources. The incomplete structure serves as a place of worship during this period.

1560:

Despite ongoing efforts to resume construction, financial challenges persist, and Cologne Cathedral remains unfinished for centuries. The structure gains the nickname "The Great Stump" due to its incomplete state.

1794:

Napoleon Bonaparte's forces occupy Cologne, and the cathedral is used as a military warehouse. The building faces significant damage during this period.

1814:

Following Napoleon's defeat, Cologne is placed under Prussian rule. Restoration efforts for the damaged cathedral commence, marking the beginning of renewed interest in completing the construction.

1842:

Architect Ernst Friedrich Zwirner is appointed to oversee the cathedral's completion. His dedication to reviving Gothic architectural principles significantly influences the cathedral's final design.

1880:

On the 14th of August, after over six centuries since the laying of the foundation stone, Cologne Cathedral is officially completed and consecrated. The twin spires make it the tallest structure in the world at the time.

World War II:

Cologne Cathedral, like many historical landmarks, suffers damage during air raids. However, it miraculously survives the bombings, earning the nickname "The Miracle of Cologne."

1956:

Restoration efforts begin to repair the damages inflicted during World War II. The intricate process involves cleaning the centuries-old stone façade and preserving the cathedral's historical integrity.

1996:

The Cologne Cathedral is designated a UNESCO World Heritage site, acknowledging its cultural and architectural significance on a global scale.

2007:

A new visitor center is inaugurated, providing tourists with additional insights into the cathedral's history, art, and architecture.

Present Day (2024):

Cologne Cathedral stands not just as a religious monument but as an enduring symbol of Cologne's resilience, architectural achievement, and cultural heritage. It continues to attract millions of visitors annually, making it one of the most iconic landmarks in Germany and Europe.

The historical timeline of Cologne Cathedral weaves a narrative of perseverance, architectural evolution, and cultural significance, spanning over seven centuries of construction, interruptions, and restoration efforts. Today, the cathedral stands tall, a testament to the dedication of those who contributed to its enduring legacy.

14.0 HEARTFELT FAREWELL BY FOLLY RAY TO TRAVELERS LEAVING COLOGNE CATHEDRAL.

Dear Adventurous Souls,

As you bid adieu to the grandeur of Cologne Cathedral, let your hearts carry not just the echoes of ancient stones but the spirit of a journey etched in time. As Folly Ray, your whimsical guide through spires and tales, I extend a heartfelt farewell, a sentiment as timeless as the cathedral itself.

You came, you marveled, and perhaps, you found a piece of your soul amid the Gothic arches and the solemn whispers of history. Cologne Cathedral, with its towering grace, has been more than a destination; it's been a companion in your exploration of the extraordinary.

As you step away, know that the cathedral's shadows will linger in your memories, reminding you of the centuries it has witnessed, the prayers it has cradled, and the travelers it has embraced. Carry the beauty of its stained glass hues and the strength of its stone walls as talismans against the mundane.

May the melodies of the bells follow you like a sweet serenade, and the panoramic views from the tower dance in your dreams. Remember the laughter of those who shared this journey with you, the whispers of history that echoed in your ears, and the moments when time stood still within those sacred walls.

Farewell, dear travelers, but let it be a "see you later" in the grand tapestry of your adventures. Cologne Cathedral's doors may close behind you, but its spirit remains an eternal companion in your wanderings.

Safe travels, and may the wonders of Cologne Cathedral continue to illuminate your path.

With heartfelt wishes,

Folly Ray

Printed in Great Britain
by Amazon

41770267R00079